Titles in the series

A SNOWY DAY
A STORMY DAY
A SUNNY DAY
A WINDY DAY

ISBN 0-86163-627-9 (cased)
ISBN 0-86163-657-0 (paperback)

Text copyright © Kate Petty 1988
Illustrations copyright © Jacqueline Wood 1988

This edition first published 1992 by
Award Publications Limited, Spring House,
Spring Place, London NW5 3BH

First published 1988 by Hodder and Stoughton
Children's Books

Printed in Singapore

All rights reserved

A STORMY DAY

Kate Petty

Illustrated by Jacqueline Wood

AWARD PUBLICATIONS

What a day!
The rain is pouring down.
Sheena watches the raindrops
running down the window.

Sheena gets ready to go out.
She puts on her raincoat,

her rainhat,

and her new red boots.

She fetches her umbrella.

Outside, the sky is dark with rain clouds. There are lights on in the houses. The pavement is wet and shiny.

Sheena likes splashing in puddles – but she hates being splashed by cars!

When it rains, drivers switch on their windscreen wipers and their headlamps.

Everybody is dripping wet. At school, Sheena takes off her outdoor clothes. She changes into dry shoes.

The children will have to play indoors today.

Plants need water to grow.
The rain soaks into the ground.
The plants suck up the water
through their roots.

Rain turns the earth to mud. The raindrops make patterns on the pond. These animals seem to like the rain.

Rainwater is rushing everywhere. It fills the gutters

and the drains,

turns streams into rivers,

and rivers into torrents as they run towards the sea.

A flash lights up the sky.
LIGHTNING! Rumble . . .
boom . . . crash!
THUNDER!

Sheena's teacher says that you see lightning before you hear thunder. This is because light travels through the air much faster than sound.

The children count 9 seconds between the next flash of lightning and the thunder which follows. That means the lightning struck 3kms away.

Lightning is a huge spark of electricity on its way from the clouds to the ground. It finds the quickest way down. Lightning conductors take it safely to earth.

A flash of lightning is very hot. It heats the air around it. The hot air expands and explodes. The noise it makes is thunder.

Animals are sometimes frightened by thunder. Thunder isn't dangerous but lightning can be.

It is best to stay away from the highest point in the area. A car is a safe place to be during a thunderstorm.

Thunder-clouds are the largest clouds of all. The tops can be 6kms up in the air. These clouds are called cumulonimbus.

Hailstones often fall from cumulonimbus clouds. Hailstones are little balls of ice. They bounce and clatter on the ground.

Rain and storms can cause a lot of damage. Heavy rain and hail spoil farmers' crops and flood their fields.

Too much rain makes the rivers rise and burst their banks. It will take a long time for these homes to dry out.

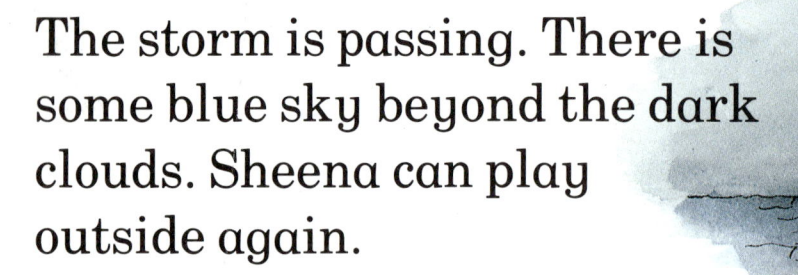

The storm is passing. There is some blue sky beyond the dark clouds. Sheena can play outside again.

Sheena turns her back to the sun and looks towards the rain. The sun shining on the raindrops makes a beautiful rainbow.

stormy day words

boots

cumulonimbus.

hail

lightning

24

puddle

rainbow

raincoat

umbrella